Original title:
Where's the Manual for This?

Copyright © 2025 Creative Arts Management OÜ
All rights reserved.

Author: Seraphina Caldwell
ISBN HARDBACK: 978-1-80566-010-1
ISBN PAPERBACK: 978-1-80566-305-8

An Open Book of Possibilities

I opened a book, thought I'd find cues,
But all I got were old-fashioned blues.
Advice on how to bake, or tame a cat,
But nothing for life—imagine that!

I flipped through the pages, searching for clues,
Found a chapter on how to tie shoes.
A recipe for soup, a yarn about ducks,
But figuring out life? Just my luck!

Each word feels like riddles, just wrinkled truths,
Sentences dancing, in mismatched boots.
I laugh at the wisdom, or lack thereof,
Seeking guidance from the stars above!

A guide for the awkward, a laugh for the lost,
In this open book, I must count the cost.
Yet still, I keep flipping, curious still,
For in every odd line, I might find a thrill!

Instructions Written in Sand

The wind blew through the pages, oh so quick,
A great idea buried, now that's a trick.
When plans dissolve in grains of golden glow,
You laugh and wonder what could go, who knows?

With every wave, new wisdom comes and goes,
Each footstep questioned where to halt or pose.
A note for travelers lost in their own jest,
The beach is fun, but, really, who knows best?

The Atlas of Ambiguity

A map with squiggly lines, I take a peek,
Direction shifts with every twist and squeak.
A legend's lost, the symbols all replaced,
Who knew that roads were such a messy space?

I check my bearings, but they seem to baffle,
"Turn left at confusion," the compass cackle.
The terrain of laughs grows wild, uncontained,
While foggy journeys keep us all entertained.

A Journey Through Unmarked Trails

With every step taken, the path feels surreal,
Nature's comedy show, what a big deal!
Around each bend, it's all slapstick fate,
The trees look down, they seem to await.

A rock sings laughter underfoot and yells,
While critters chuckle, sharing their tales.
Lost in the giggles of unpaved delight,
Adventure awaits when the map is just light.

Improvise: The Only Option

With props of nonsense, we start the grand play,
Winging it boldly, come what may.
Directions are folly, spontaneity reigns,
Laughter erupts, releasing our chains.

Ad-libbed solutions, chaos takes flight,
In this wild comedy, everything's right.
So grab your quirks, let's dance through the night,
Who needs instructions when fun's in our sight?

The Sound of Unwritten Stories

Whispers from the pages, unturned,
A plot twist here, a tale that's burned.
Characters dance, but no one can tell,
How to wring laughter from this living shell.

Footnotes scribbled, half-baked affairs,
Chasing bright ideas as if they were chairs.
With scripts unwritten, chaos unfolds,
In the world of the brave, the bold, and the olds.

On a Tightrope of Guesswork

Balancing life with a wink and a smile,
Tiptoeing through puzzles that stretch every mile.
Every misstep, a chance to have fun,
While laughing at logic that's nowhere to run.

Each day's a riddle, a playful stunt,
Trying to untangle the wild and the blunt.
With every trip, there's a giggle or two,
In a circus of choices, what's a clown to do?

Sailing with No Star

Drifting on waters of wild imagination,
With no guiding light, just pure fascination.
The compass spins wild in a fog of delight,
As we chase silly dreams through the starless night.

Oh, the waves laugh as we sail off course,
Finding treasure in nonsense, a powerful force.
With each splash, we toss reason overboard,
In a frenzy of chaos, where laughter is stored.

Resonance of the Unfamed

Echoes of voices that don't make the chart,
Bouncing on rhythms that dance from the heart.
In the realm of the awkward, the heroes arise,
Crafting their stories in whimsical skies.

The unheard tales bring a chuckle, a cheer,
Making fun of the things that we all hold dear.
In a world without rules, adventure awaits,
With a wink to the future, and all its shapes.

The Whisper of Unspoken Rules

In a world full of signs, I'm lost at sea,
Instructions scribbled, but none left for me.
The coffee's too strong, the soup's way too hot,
And every small task is a puzzling plot.

I trip on the mat, then dance like a fool,
A clown in the cereal, that's just how I roll.
With winks and with nods, we all share the game,
Yet no one can tell me just how to play the same.

The keys in the fridge, the phone in my shoe,
Like circus acrobats, my thoughts tumble too.
I smile through the chaos, laugh through the strife,
These quirky mishaps are just part of life.

Though guides may be missing, I'm learning to jest,
In a world of confusion, I'll give it my best.
With giggles and snorts, I embrace every fall,
For in the end, it's a great show for all.

Trials and Errors of the Heart

I sent a sweet text, but hit 'send' too late,
Turns out my sweet crush now finds me quite straight.
I trip on my words, and my heart starts to race,
Playing tag with feelings, oh, what a wild chase.

I bought flowers bright, but forgot the card,
My date thinks I'm strange, and the evening's quite hard.
Yet over warm pizza, we chuckle and share,
Found laughter's sweet balm, to mend every scare.

Missteps are plenty, like trying to dance,
I step on her toes, oh, isn't love a chance?
Yet each little goof makes the moment more real,
In this game of the heart, it's the laughter we feel.

With stumbles and laughter, the night rolls on fast,
The awkwardness lingers, but how could it last?
For while there's no guide on this whimsical ride,
It's the joy from the trials that bloom as our pride.

An Odyssey Without Directions

My GPS says, 'You've arrived at your fate,'
But I'm clearly still lost, isn't that just great?
With a map folded wrong and a snack in my pack,
I venture on roads that twist and then crack.

I asked for the way; they pointed and grinned,
Their advice? Quite sketchy, like where to begin.
Through valleys of doubt, I wander and stumble,
With every misstep, my confidence crumbles.

I meet a lost llama, we share a bemused stare,
Who knew adventure came with such flair?
We laugh at the signs that just spin round and round,
In this maze of a journey, fun's what we found.

Through hills that won't yield, and paths never tread,
I'm writing my story, with giggles instead.
For while there are no maps to guide what's ahead,
It's the laughter that leads where curiosity's led.

Unraveled Threads of Uncertainty

In a life full of colors, I've picked up the grey,
Tangled up wool makes a fine mess of play.
Socks mismatched and lost, and sweaters go askew,
Each thread tells a story; oh, what will ensue?

With needles that clack like an orchestra gone,
I try to make sense, but the yarns all conspire.
They twist and they tangle, a true artistic crime,
Yet somehow I'm giggling, like I'm lost in rhyme.

A scarf turns out cosmic, a blanket quite short,
My fashion's a circus, a whimsical sport.
Each knot tells a joke, every pull makes me sigh,
My wardrobe's a riddle; oh, how time does fly.

As threads unravel, my laughter will grow,
In this tangled chaot, I'm putting on a show.
For while I may wander with no guiding thread,
It's the fun in the fray that fills me instead.

The Silent Manual of Experiences

I woke up one day, what a surprise,
The alarm went off, but I closed my eyes.
Instructions unclear, am I late for the show?
Or did I just dream of a life on the go?

Coffee spill on my shirt, it's a fashion choice,
But my reflection seems to shout, 'You've lost your voice!'
Baking a cake, but forgot the flour,
Now it's a pancake—life's bizarre power!

Texting my mom, 'What do I do?'
She replies with a meme—great, thanks for the clue!
Journey continues, each step is a trip,
Navigating chaos, just trying to grip.

Every mishap, a lesson dropped,
These silent guides are where I've flopped.
Yet here I am, and I've had some fun,
Learning through laughter, we've only begun.

Misprints in the Book of Life

Opened the first page, what do I see?
Printed in bold, 'Be all that you can be!'
Turned to chapter two, and what do I find?
A recipe for socks? Oh, I've lost my mind!

'List your top goals!' it prompts with delight,
But then I forgot them, and it's already night.
In this comic book, the storyline bends,
It seems every lesson needs a few friends.

Read about love, tiptoed on fate,
But all I discovered was my cat on the crate.
With each line that prints, things look askew,
But who needs a plan when donuts are due?

So here I stand, in a whirlwind of cheer,
Embracing the typos that brought me here.
Flipping thick pages, I laugh at my strife,
Misprints and doodles, this is my life.

Charting the Unexplored

Got a map that's blank, like my morning fate,
A dotted line drawing, oh why did I wait?
Some say adventure is calling my name,
But I'm stuck in the fridge, playing the game!

Off to find treasure, or maybe just snacks,
With a potato as compass, I swear I'll relax.
Each twist and each turn leads to giggles galore,
Lost in my backyard, but what's worth the score?

The map gives me hints—thoughts all in code,
But the X that I found just led to my abode.
Exploration means stepping out of the norm,
Where shadows are real, but that's part of the charm.

Together with friends, we're charting the fun,
In a world so confusing, yet brightly it's spun.
Uncharted hearts mapping giggles and glee,
Navigating nonsense, just you wait and see!

The Code Beneath Our Skin

They say the heart speaks in a language so rare,
But mine just mutters, 'Do you have a spare?'
Seeking the manual, it's bound up so tight,
As feelings get tangled in a long, silly fight.

My brain writes in riddles, it's a puzzle, I swear,
With snacks as the punchline—it's really unfair!
Love is a cipher, and friendship's a joke,
I'm cracking the code, but it's all just smoke.

Scrolling through moments, I try to decipher,
Yet messages bounce, like a cat with a cypher.
In laughter and quirks, we find our own rules,
Confusing as math, yet here are the fools!

So dance to the rhythm of who we are meant,
Decode with a smile, let's pay up the rent!
In the code of our being, we find what we seek,
Together in madness, we laugh and we speak.

The Script We Never Wrote

We fumble through each line, it's true,
Unsure of what we're meant to do.
The plot twists in the funniest ways,
As we improvise our clumsy plays.

With characters that change their names,
And earnest goals that feel like games.
Each scene a mix of old and new,
The laughter flows, our fears too few.

So grab a pen, let's scribble fast,
We'll weave a tale that's built to last.
We'll write our story with a grin,
And let the chaos then begin!

In the end, it matters not the art,
But all the fun we had to start.
The joy of wings on failure's flight,
In this wild script, we find our light.

When Certainty Is an Illusion

I woke up sure it was a Friday,
Only to find it's Sunday, yay!
My schedule laughed, my plans took flight,
As I danced to this surprise delight.

With coffee spilling on the floor,
I question life, but want much more.
The clock ticks on a rhythm strange,
While certainty begins to change.

I check my phone for signs and clues,
But end up scrolling silly news.
On days like these, I guess it's true,
The only guide is laughter too!

So here's to chaos, joy, and cheer,
Embrace the mess, shed every fear.
In doubt, we often find what's real,
A comedy spun from the surreal.

An Odyssey with No Roadmap

In a car with no GPS to guide,
We set out for a joyful ride.
Each turn a mystery, every lane,
As laughter fills the air like rain.

Lost in fields where cows just stare,
Our destination? Well, who cares?
With snacks piled high, and tunes so bright,
We wander till the stars ignite.

Google Maps… we tossed aside,
Instead we take the wacky ride.
Each wrong turn becomes a tale,
Of mishaps and mischief, we prevail!

So steer away from paths pre-set,
The joy of getting lost? You bet!
In every twist and every turn,
New adventures for which we yearn.

The Incremental Guide to Growth

Step by step, we climb the hill,
With every small win, we feel the thrill.
Like plants that stretch toward the sun,
In tiny moments, life is won.

At times we trip, we stumble back,
Yet still we laugh, no need to slack.
With growth charts that look like art,
Each mark a sign, each stroke a part.

We plant our seeds with hopeful hearts,
In this green space, we play our parts.
With water, sunshine, love, and care,
The quirks of life unfold somewhere.

So let the journey be your guide,
In increments, let dreams collide.
Through every laugh, we learn and thrive,
In this show of wits, we come alive.

Scripted by Serendipity

Life's a script, yet pages stall,
With every line, I trip and fall.
I check the plot, but it's all a mess,
Turns out, I'm just here to guess.

From coffee spills to missteps galore,
I'm not sure what's behind that door.
The stage is set, the actors too,
But who wrote this? Not a clue!

I dance like no one sees my plight,
With hidden moves in the spotlight,
The cue cards blank, a lovely jest,
Turns out, fun's my only quest.

Each twist, a laugh in disguise,
Learning life through silly tries.
If I had a script, I'd bid it adieu,
For chaos is the best debut!

The Cartographer's Dilemma

A map appears, but wait… what's this?
X marks the spot, but where's my bliss?
I've got a compass, but it spins around,
    Directions? Lost, without a sound.

    I charted seas, but none resemble,
    The land I seek, oh how I tremble.
    Each fold a riddle, a jigsaw mess,
        Adventure calls, so let's confess!

    The rivers swirl, a laugh so grand,
    I'm on my way to a foreign land.
If signs could talk, they'd surely mock,
    For I'm just here, a wayward dock.

Yet joy unfolds in every wrong turn,
Finding treasure where candles burn.
    The quest itself is quite the lure,
And who needs maps when fun's the cure?

In the Absence of Directions

Maps are confusing, a labyrinth wide,
No arrows pointed, nowhere to hide.
I wander forth with a grin on my face,
In the chaos, I find my place.

Road signs shiver, but I don't care,
With each wrong turn, I find fresh air.
The wayward path is simply divine,
Who knew detours would lead to wine?

I'm lost but look, there's ice cream near!
In every mishap, I find some cheer.
If life's the journey, then let it unspool,
With laughs aplenty, I'll play the fool.

The path may twist and the stakes may rise,
But with whimsy as my trusty guise,
A heart that laughs is free and bold,
In absence of rules, life's gold unfolds.

Brewed in the Unknown

A pot of coffee, I brew with care,
But somehow I've spilled it everywhere.
The recipe's gone, a sight to behold,
Yet laughter brews better than gold.

I whisk my dreams in a frothy spree,
With each soggy sip, I'm wild and free.
The beans revolt, doing their dance,
I take a sip, and oh—what a chance!

Each cup is a mystery, a scrumptious fight,
I'm tasting chaos, it's pure delight.
Espresso shots and fumbles divine,
This unscripted blend? A rare design.

So fill up my mug with love and delight,
In the unknown, I'll find what's right.
With every pour, the giggles flow,
Who needs a manual? Let's just go!

An Expedition Without a Map

This journey leads us far and wide,
We're driving with no place to hide.
The compass spins, a wild charade,
While squirrels laugh at plans we've made.

The GPS gave out at mile five,
Without an ounce of hope to thrive.
We'll dance with fate, and twist in turns,
Finding treasure in our goofy yearns.

Who needs a guide? Let's roam instead!
With stories that tickle, words to spread.
In this chaos, laughter's the key,
Let's chart our course, just you and me.

Treading on Unfamiliar Ground

A shoe fell off, it didn't belong,
Two left feet in a tango wrong.
We trip and stumble, a merry sight,
Like clowns at a circus, take off in flight.

Each step feels like a slapstick show,
With wobbly strides, we put on a glow.
The ground shakes, but we'll never fall,
Giggles explode, and we stand tall.

Our map's a scribble on a napkin stained,
Lost in laughter, we boldly remained.
With every misstep, we find our groove,
On this strange road, we learn to move.

Pages Torn from the Manual

We search for hints in crumpled sheets,
Each page we find raises new feats.
Instructions written in an old code,
Make a salad or hit the road?

One line suggests a chicken dance,
Another warns: "Never take a chance!"
With piecemeal wisdom, we roll our eyes,
And turn our errors into sweet surprise.

Thumbing through, what's next to try?
A recipe for laughter, pie in the sky.
In this disarray, we found our fun,
Life's quirky class has just begun!

The If and When of Living

If you trip while trying to blend,
Just laugh, my friend, it's all in the trend.
When life throws curves, become the jest,
Inquirers of joy, we give it our best.

If the sun won't shine, get out your shades,
Dance in the puddles, life's playful glades.
When worry creeps in like an unwelcome sprout,
Just tickle its fancy and laugh it out.

The secret to living? Simply embrace,
Each moment's a riddle, just pick up the pace.
If and when blend into a cheer,
With giggles and grins, we'll persevere.

Trial and Error: My Daily Journey

Woke up thinking I'd be wise,
Only to trip on my own ties.
Coffee spilled, my shirt's a mess,
Guess today's a fun-filled test!

I tried to cook, burnt the toast,
Called the dog, he was my host.
A dance in the kitchen, chips on the floor,
This life is a circus, a slapstick encore!

The phone rings, who could it be?
Oh right, it's just my own sneeze spree!
Passwords forgotten, dog ate the clue,
If only I had a guide for this too!

But laughter helps when plans go wrong,
Life's a puzzle, dance along!
Turns out chaos has its charms,
With errors that may raise alarms!

The Outdated Atlas of Emotion

Turned a page and lost my way,
Heart's compass brakes, it won't play.
Maps of feelings, slightly worn,
Torn edges say, "Why were you born?"

A tickle meant a burst of cheer,
But is it laughter or just a sneeze near?
I reach for joy, I grab for tears,
Navigating life could fuel my fears!

I stumbled on love, it felt like a game,
But what's the score? Is it all the same?
A guide to feelings would be alright,
Instead, I'm lost in a ping-pong fight!

But here's a map made of dreams,
Where emotions burst like silly streams.
So I'll just laugh and take a chance,
Trust that life's a rollicking dance!

Recipes for Unforeseen Moments

Take a pinch of zest and fun,
Mix in mischief, just begun.
Add a dollop of what-ifs, bold,
Stir until the chaos unfolds!

Sprinkle in laughter, toss in a dash,
A real-life drama turned to a clash.
Bake for hours, 'til bright ideas rise,
Serve with a side of playful surprise!

A pinch of doubt, a splash of hope,
Mixing flavors that help me cope.
Add chocolate chips for a sweet laugh,
Here's your recipe—no need for a graph!

So whip it up, don't read the rules,
Life's a kitchen, we're just the fools.
Taste here, and there, create your art,
For unforeseen moments, play your part!

Unfolding the Enigma of Us

Two jigsaw pieces, oddly shaped,
We fit together, yet escape.
One day sweet, the next a fright,
Our story twists, left and right!

A puzzle box with missing bits,
Each laugh a clue, amidst the wits.
Your favorite color's still a guess,
And socks misplaced, I won't confess!

I asked for sushi, got veggie stew,
Dinner dates, oh what to do?
Instructions lost, but it's alright,
In this odd dance, we find our light!

So hand in hand, we futz and fumble,
Through each twist, we joyfully tumble.
The enigma's fun, let's take a chance,
In this riddle of life, let's laugh and dance!

Whispers of the Unsure Path

In the drawer of my brain lies a mess,
Like socks without a mate, I confess.
I wander through life with no clear plan,
Each step's a surprise, like a wild game of Scran.

Maps are for others, not for my fate,
I'm turning left where the signs say 'wait'.
Shaking my head at the wisdom I lack,
Life's just a puzzle, and I lost the pack.

They say to stay straight where the arrows point,
But I zig and zag, like a joyfully anointed.
If laughter's the guide, then I'll surely thrive,
A footloose dance, oh, how I survive!

So here's to the twists, the turns, the falls,
To giggling through chaos, and strange bathroom stalls.
Each blunder a story, each fumble a cheer,
In this game of life, I'll stick it, never fear!

Scribbled Notes on Living

With crumpled papers tossed all around,
I scribble my thoughts, but they're lost, never found.
'Follow your heart'—that line seems so sweet,
But it leads to the chocolate aisle, oh what a feat!

Instructions for dinner, I'll wing it tonight,
Burnt pasta and winks, that's my kind of bite.
They say keep it simple, so I added some flair,
A pinch of confusion, go ahead, take a dare!

Life hacks abound, whispered in crowds,
But none quite as fun as dancing in clouds.
With every misstep, I learn something new,
Like wearing mismatched shoes makes life less blue.

So here's to the chaos in each scribbled line,
To the cool kids of life, who redefine.
Drawn in bright markers, our stories unfold,
Cheesy and giggly, that's how we roll!

Lost Instructions for the Heart

My heart's a GPS with no signal in sight,
It says 'recalculating' in the middle of the night.
I text it for answers, it shrugs with a sigh,
Love's just a riddle that makes me ask 'why?'

It's like pie without filling, a joke without punch,
A game of charades at a messy old brunch.
With feelings that flip like pancakes at dawn,
I rise with a smile, 'cause laughter's my song.

Trying to read the map written in sand,
I misinterpret love, it's not what I planned.
A tango with timing, a flip in the air,
But it's funny to tumble, and that's half the care.

So here's to the mystery, the rhythm, the spark,
To dancing through heartache, and laughing in dark.
In friendship and folly, all tangled and sweet,
Let's toast to the journey, it's quite the treat!

Unwritten Guidelines of Life

A blank book lies open, its pages so clean,
I'm drawing my roadmap with crayons unseen.
The teacher said 'focus', but look where I strayed,
Life's a messy playground where laughter's the trade.

No chapters, no verses, just friendly advice,
I follow the butterflies, oh they're so nice!
Turn left at the rainbow, drink tea with a cloud,
The rules are all nonsense, let's dance in a crowd.

Epic fails become stories we tell,
Like that time with the llama—that went really well!
Each 'oops' a reminder of joy in the strife,
The unwritten guidelines are part of this life.

So sit back and giggle at plans thrown away,
For each twist in the road brings a fresh light of day.
Raise a glass to the laughter, the whims, the wild tide,
In this lovely chaos, let's take it in stride!

Lost in the Instructions of Life

I opened the manual, but it was blank,
A cosmic joke, or maybe just pranks.
Instructions in riddles, or so it seems,
Life's like a puzzle, torn at the seams.

I flipped to a section, but what do I find?
A drawing of sushi? Is this out of line?
I tried to assemble the pieces with care,
But all I got was a mustache of hair.

There's no table of contents for how to get by,
Just a bunch of sticky notes and a pie in the sky.
Why aren't there warnings for heavy lifting love?
They left out the chapters on feeling the shove.

So here I am, lost in the whims of it all,
With no user guide to catch me if I fall.
I'll laugh at the hiccups, the trials and the blights,
And dance to the rhythm of my own silly sights.

The Guidebook in My Pocket

I've got a pocket guide, it's tattered and torn,
It shows how to cook, but I'm still forlorn.
Step one says 'chop,' then it goes 'take a break,'
But fries are on fire, how much can one take?

I stumbled upon a chapter on romance,
But it read like a sitcom, not leaving me chance.
"Flirt with a glance, but don't spill your drink,"
Now I'm stuck in a moment, just trying to think.

The travel tips say to always pack light,
But my suitcase is bursting — it's quite a sight!
With flip-flops and wigs, and a clown nose too,
Why did I pack up my whole zoo?

Yet in all the chaos, I find a great cheer,
The guidebook's a giggle, it feels like a beer.
So I'll scratch out the rules and rewrite the plan,
Turns out there's wisdom in not being a man.

Navigating Without a Map

I set out for dinner, my phone lost its signal,
Thought I'd just wing it, but it felt quite cynical.
A left at the old tree, two rights near the park,
Who knew that I'd end up lost in the dark?

With each wrong turn, I meet quirky sights,
A chicken in pajamas, oh what a delight!
The squirrels are my tour guides, they wave from the trees,
Inviting me in for a round of warm cheese.

A map in my hand, but the ink's running low,
I might as well follow the firefly glow.
Each street is a laughter; each bump is a jest,
If I'm lost on my journey, well, isn't that best?

So I wander and wonder with glee in my heart,
Here's to the maze that became its own art.
With twists and with turns leading me to a laugh,
Forget the map, I'm just chasing the path!

Unwritten Rules of the Heart

Love's got its quirks, like a dance with no tune,
I asked for the steps, but they vanished too soon.
"Be charming," they said, but what does that mean?
My charm's like a puppy — all goofy and green.

It's said to be gentle, but push and then pull,
The heart is a whirlpool, ever so full.
One moment it sparkles, the next it can sting,
A baffling carnival, the wildest of swings.

In whispers and giggles, it ebbs and it flows,
While my heart plays hide and seek with my toes.
There's no cheat sheet for passion in flight,
Just a tickle of joy, a snort, and a bite.

So here's to the laughter, the twists and the bends,
To the unwritten rules and the love that transcends.
For in all of its chaos, I find my own art,
Mixing giggles and winks in the rules of the heart.

Beyond the Map's Edge

Lost in the land of the unknown,
A compass that spins like a drone.
I ask for directions with flair,
But locals just grin, unaware.

My phone's dead, GPS on strike,
I choose to follow a passing bike.
With each step, my courage does leap,
No map in my pocket, just hope in my keep.

A sign by a tree, it says 'Beware!'
Of what, I just can't seem to compare.
The path unclear, I dance in delight,
Turns out it's a shortcut to fright!

Adventures unfold, oh what a spree,
I tripped on a root, now laughing with glee.
No guidebook to follow, no rules to break,
Just me and the wild, for fun's own sake!

Crumpled Pages of Experience

Gather around as I tell my tale,
Of journeys embarked, and trials that fail.
Pages so crumpled, like my poor shoes,
Lessons in laughter, come hear my muse!

I packed all the snacks, forgot all the gear,
A fine balance of joy mixed with fear.
The tent poles were lost, the sun took a dive,
But who needs a tent? We'll just sleep outside!

Each crumpled note tells stories untold,
Of getting lost while feeling so bold.
I tried to cook pasta, you should've seen,
A fireball frenzy, it wasn't serene!

So here's to the trips with no proper plan,
To mishaps and laughter and infinite fun.
The only manual I truly demand,
Is one that serves snacks and comes with a pun!

A Script Not Yet Penned

A journey unfolds with no script in sight,
Wandering clueless, yet feeling so right.
My suitcase has wheels, my heart has a song,
With each twist and turn, I just tag along.

I've joined a parade, donned a strange hat,
Danced with a llama, oh imagine that!
The locals just chuckle, oh what a crew,
They know that it's freer when you haven't a clue.

I tried to decipher a menu so grand,
With items I can't pronounce or understand.
But laughter erupted - oh what a treat,
As I ordered a dish meant to eat with your feet!

In this script unwritten, let chaos reign,
Mix joy with confusion, dance in the rain.
For every misstep, there's fun to be had,
In this grand play of life, here's to being mad!

Tales of the Unprepared Traveler

With sandals and socks, I'm ready to roam,
No itinerary made, just leave it at home.
Maps are for planners, I'm winging it free,
My only advice? Bring snacks, not a key!

Didn't check weather, surprise, here's the storm,
Drenched like a sponge, still I feel warm.
A duck quacks my name, I waddle along,
With each silly step, I create a new song.

I stomped in the puddles, splashed all around,
In laughter and joy, my spirit is found.
No guidebook, no targets, just pure silly fun,
Adventure is calling, and I've just begun!

So here's to the travelers, unprepared and bold,
With stories to share that never grow old.
With humor our compass, and whimsy our map,
We'll treasure the journey, let's take a nap!

A Path Through Shadows

In the dark, I trip and fall,
I'd rather not, but here we are at all.
A sign, a clue, where could it be?
Just me and my shadow, what a sight to see.

Every turn, a laugh or a shout,
They say it's fun, I am filled with doubt.
I dance with a branch, it hits me back,
No map in hand, I'm off the track.

A squirrel giggles, clearly amused,
I wave hello, I'm not confused.
Is it left or right? I can't quite tell,
My feet are weary, I bid farewell.

Yet here I roam, a traveler bold,
In this playful maze, not books of old.
For every wrong turn, let laughter sing,
In shadows we find the joy life brings.

The Unscripted Adventure

With no guidebook, what could go wrong?
I step out bravely, humming a song.
A coffee spill, oh what a scene,
This unscripted life, my favorite routine.

In the market, I lose my way,
Peddlers shout, "Come buy, okay?"
I barter with snacks, a silly trade,
A hat for a donut, in laughter I wade.

Wandering paths with shoes untied,
Every stumble, a joyful ride.
I meet a cat, he rolls in style,
That's the true map, a friendly smile.

So here I am, in chaos sweet,
No manual needed, on my own two feet.
Each moment's a page, scrawled down in ink,
In this wacky tale, I'm happy to think.

Fog in the Pathway Ahead

The mist rolls in, all paths obscure,
I squint and grin, adventure's allure.
Step left or right? The fog does sway,
A whimsical game, let's hope I'll stay.

Voices call out from nowhere near,
Is it a friend or the wind I hear?
I chuckle aloud, this game of hide,
In foggy realms, it's fun to glide.

I chase after footsteps that lead to nowhere,
Stumbling around, in fresh, chilly air.
Every twist brings giggles and gasps,
Laughter echoes as clarity clasps.

At last, a hint, a beacon of light,
Through all the fog, I'm feeling all right.
For in the mist, joy's found today,
With laughs and quips, I'll find my way.

Searching for Clarity in a Tangle

Tangled thoughts, like vines they grow,
I snip away at what I know.
Each flustered turn, a comical sight,
Where clarity hides, wrapped up tight.

My brain's a maze, a jumbled thread,
I untangle dreams, both silly and red.
A light bulb flickers, almost there,
Half-formed thoughts dance in the air.

I wave to confusion, it waves back slow,
In this quirky game, we steal the show.
Every question leads to a grin,
In this tangled web, let the fun begin.

So here I am, in chaos grand,
With laughter's light, I take a stand.
Searching for clarity? Oh what a quest,
In this beautiful tangle, I am blessed.

The Art of Uncharted Living

Lost in a sea of simple tasks,
A guide would be great, but who ever asks?
My socks don't match, but that's okay,
Life's an adventure, come what may.

Fried eggs are a gamble, a toss of the pan,
I cook like a pro, or at least I can.
Instructions unclear, all's well that bends,
In this wild ride, it's just me and my friends.

Maps are for others, I wander alone,
With coffee as compass, I make it my own.
A recipe's fine, but I'll wing the rest,
In this game of life, I'm simply bemessed.

So here's to the chaos, the norm I defy,
Laughing through mishaps, giving it a try.
No rulebook in sight, just moments to savor,
In the art of uncharted, I find all my flavor.

Confessions of a Confused Voyager

I took a wrong turn, but who keeps track?
Maps are all gone, I'm lost in the black.
With Google in my pocket, still wandering free,
Life's real journey is thrilling to me.

A coffee shop haunt turns into a maze,
Barista speaks fast, I'm lost in a daze.
I nod and I smile, pretending I'm wise,
But oh, what they mean just confounds my eyes.

Missed the last exit, but that was my plan,
Life's a sitcom, so let's rerun it, man.
With laughter as fuel, I'll stumble along,
In the show of confusion, I'll dance to my song.

Every wrong turn is a leap into fate,
Fate's got jokes, oh, isn't it great?
Join in my story, be part of the mess,
As a confused voyager, I feel truly blessed.

Instructions Left Unseen

Found a box labeled 'for dummies', oh dear,
Opened it up, but lost all my cheer.
With parts and with gadgets, I fumble and fight,
Making a toaster just doesn't feel right.

Who needs a manual when Wi-Fi is here?
Google says, 'Try it!' but I can't steer clear.
It cooks my breakfast or simply explodes,
In this world of 'what ifs', anything erodes.

My plants are a puzzle, they wilt at my touch,
I water them wrong, but I care so much.
'Indoor foliage' seems like a faraway land,
With each leaf that droops, I try to understand.

So throw out the manual, dive in the fray,
I'm building my chaos in my own clever way.
With each blunder I make, I find something new,
Instructions unseen, but I'm learning from you.

The User's Guide to the Unknown

Once I sought answers, but lost all my notes,
Now I improvise life with mismatched quotes.
If wisdom is grand, I'm missing the class,
Juggling these thoughts like a clown with a glass.

Should I spin it left, or perhaps give a twist?
Muddled my choices, can't say I'm a whiz.
The path isn't clear, but hey, it's all fun,
Kites in the wind, oh, look how they run!

Chasing the sunset, with snacks in my pack,
I'm mapping the stars, but the sky's pitch black.
If all fails gloriously, let laughter be loud,
In the guide to the unknown, I'll wear my crown proud.

So here's to the journey, however it goes,
When life hands you lemons, just follow your nose.
With no user's guide, and that's perfectly fine,
In this wacky adventure, I'll dance the divine.

Umbral Insights

In the dark, I search about,
Wishing for a hint or shout.
Instructions lost, they went in vain,
I laugh while spinning in my brain.

Those screws are slippery, what a pain!
Do I twist or pull, or should I feign?
With every turn, my heart does race,
Is there a guide for this wild chase?

Shiny things are nice to touch,
But often they're the ones that clutch.
I poke and prod, with much surprise,
My clumsiness, a grand disguise.

In the end, I've turned a knob,
It leads to chaos, jobbed my job.
Who knew a dance was on the floor?
With laughter, I'm lost forevermore.

In Search of Clarity's Light

With foggy thoughts, I roam the halls,
Each echo answers with baffling calls.
I follow signs that make no sense,
Like finding clues in a misty fence.

Coffee cups and tangled sheets,
Instructions buried 'neath my feets.
A map in scribbles, I try to read,
But it's a recipe for more misdeed.

Round the corner, there's a door,
But who can say what's there in store?
A helpful hint would do me right,
Instead, I plunge into the night.

At every turn, there's laughter's spark,
For clarity's light seems just too stark.
I wave goodbye to all my woes,
In search of clarity, where confusion grows.

The Labyrinth of Intuition

In a maze with twists and bends,
My intuition teases, never lends.
I talk to walls, and they just sigh,
"Why don't you just try to fly?"

Tangled routes and slippery roads,
Who knew wisdom bore such loads?
I ask the air, "Can you assist?"
It chuckles back, too much on the list.

Left or right? It's anyone's guess,
Adventure turns to a glorious mess.
Each step I take, I trip and roll,
A circus act becomes my goal.

In this labyrinth, I laugh and play,
For wrong turns often lead the way.
With confusion painted bright and bold,
I'll find the treasure, or so I'm told.

The Beacons of Unknowing

Bright beacons flash, but what's the cue?
I squint and wonder, "Is it true?"
Navigating paths both wide and narrow,
Like chasing shadows, my own sparrow.

A map with smudges tells tall tales,
Of dreaded dragons and windy gales.
With little guidance, I'm set afloat,
On a ship that's sprung a leaky boat.

Each light a riddle, a lovely tease,
As I juggle doubts with utmost ease.
What's around that glowing bend?
Is it wisdom, or a cheeky friend?

With laughter bright and spirits high,
I wander forth beneath the sky.
In the beacons of unknowing, I find,
The joy of mystery intertwined.

Words Chiseled in Clouds

I asked the clouds for wisdom stashed,
They just floated by, completely dashed.
With every question aimed so high,
The answers giggled, then waved goodbye.

I scribbled notes on the breeze's fate,
The wind just chuckled, a teasing mate.
Each thought I caught slipped through my grasp,
Like wisps of dreams in a playful rasp.

I built a ladder to reach the sun,
But tripped on nothing—oh, what fun!
The sky won't tell me what I need,
Yet here I float, a joyful steed.

In this absurdity I find my glee,
Chasing ideas that run wild and free.
Though lost, I dance with a heart that's light,
Laughing through questions into the night.

The Quill in My Hand

With a quill in hand, I start to write,
But the ink spills out, oh what a sight!
Words take flight, but where do they go?
A riddle wrapped in a feathered show.

Each stroke a puzzle, a loop and a spin,
My thoughts escape like a giddy grin.
Pages are filled with absurdity's twist,
Like trying to find a truth in a mist.

I search for directions in every dot,
But all I find is a paper knot.
So I doodle a cat riding a whale,
Laughing out loud at my own funny tale.

Though clarity hides, I'm still having fun,
In this quizzical journey, I won't be outdone.
For laughter's the ink that colors my day,
In the chaos of words, I'll find my own way.

Essence of the Unsure Journey

I packed my bag with a pinch of fear,
And set off hoping for a treasure near.
With sticky notes stuck to my sleeve,
I search for signs like a well-worn sleeve.

The map I drew looks like a doodle,
Leading me to a giant poodle.
Each turn is a giggle, a mishap, a laugh,
In this maze of life, I take the wrong path.

I ask for guidance, the stars just wink,
And I tumble down, leaving me to think.
With each bumble, I trip on delight,
In the journey of guess, I find what feels right.

Though unplanned, I glide with flair,
Embracing the joy of the unaware.
For in every blunder, there's wisdom unspun,
Crafted from laughter, oh what fun!

The Infinite Questions Within

Questions dance in my crowded head,
Like a party where logic has fled.
They twirl and spin, then jump on the floor,
Demanding attention, but I'm keeping score.

Each riddle pops like a bubble, see?
In the circus of thoughts, there's no decree.
With each puzzled look, I give them a grin,
Embracing the chaos that's brewing within.

I query the moon about the sun's great glare,
But it just laughs, with no answer to share.
I'm lost in a labyrinth, yet giggling low,
As questions become my shrinking shadow.

So I gather these quirks, these whimsical quests,
And toss them around like confetti at best.
For in every question, there's laughter and play,
Just another adventure to brighten my day.

The Quest for Invisible Signs

Lost in a maze of clues sublime,
Every corner turned, I lose more time.
Guessing the arrows, where do they point?
A riddle wrapped in a snack bar joint.

Balloons float high, maps look absurd,
I follow a squirrel, a wise little bird.
With breadcrumbs of hope, I try to track,
But even the breadcrumbs have started to snack.

Puzzles and giggles, life's odd ballet,
Why's nobody laughing at my grand display?
With each wrong turn, I find new delight,
Maybe the answers are hidden from sight.

So here's to the journey, the chuckles I've found,
In this quest for the signs, I'm more lost than bound.
I'll dance in the chaos, I'll sing in the rain,
Maybe the fun is the grandest of gains.

Guidelines Made of Mist

I woke up today, thought I'd take a peek,
Hoping for guidance, but all I see is bleak.
Instructions in fog, how strange could it be?
A map made of whispers, not meant for me.

Fluffy clouds float by, with suggestions to heed,
Navigational llamas, were those in my creed?
I scribble in air with my invisible pen,
Though I'm guided by laughter, again and again.

Detours through laughter, I'm lost in delight,
Each twist and each turn, brings more silly sights.
With every misstep, I giggle and cling,
To the joy of the journey, that's the dance I bring.

So let go of the rules, and roll with the fun,
In this fog-filled maze, I'll still be the one.
Guidelines of mist fade, but joy's here to stay,
In this quirky adventure, I'll find my own way.

Finding Light in the Unknown

In the shadows of doubt, I tiptoe with flair,
Holding a lantern that lights up the air.
What's hidden in chaos? What's squirming beneath?
A glittery puppy or a lost golden wreath?

The path is a dance, a waltz with surprise,
I search for my fortune, beneath metaphorical skies.
Is it candy or wisdom that calls out my name?
In the theater of mystery, it's all just a game.

I wade through the silly, the absurd and the wild,
As the universe chuckles, like a playful child.
With each silly stutter, there's joy to juggle,
I embrace the unknown and unwrap all the muddle.

So here's to the moments we can't quite define,
In the light of the laughter, the fun's all mine.
I'll keep spinning in circles, a giggling storm,
Finding joy in the dark, cozy, and warm.

The Book of Unawarded Wisdom

Tucked between pages of half-baked advice,
Is a wisdom so quirky, it's oh-so-nice.
Chapter One whispers, 'eat cake for your woes,'
While Chapter Two chuckles, 'never trust moles.'

An ode to absurd, with each turn of the page,
This book full of nonsense, is all the rage.
Every tale more ludicrous than the last,
Spinning laughter like a whimsical cast.

I scribble in margins, my thoughts fly away,
Grab my rubber chicken, let's frolic and play.
With wisdom unawarded, I embrace the weird,
In the land of the silly, my heart's never steered.

So here's to the nonsense that makes spirits rise,
Life's quirkiest gems shine bright in disguise.
In this book of confusion, where laughter sets free,
I'll wear my crown of joy, just let me be me.

The Art of Wandering Blind

In a world of twists and turns,
I tried to glance ahead,
But with each step I take,
I'm lost without a thread.

With socks that don't quite match,
And shoes upon the wrong feet,
I dance like I'm on par,
To a tune that's quite obsolete.

I asked a tree for guidance,
It rustled with delight,
But bark won't give directions,
Guess I'll keep up this fight.

So here's to fumbling forward,
With no compass in my hand,
It's clearer with each stumble,
Life's just a wonderland.

Blueprint of the Uncertain

My DIY dreams take shape,
But no tools are close at hand,
I look at all the pieces,
Doubt starts to expand.

Instructions lost in chaos,
A puzzle's got me stumped,
Is this a chair or spaceship?
Oh dear, my pride is plumped!

The hammer swings in shock,
The nails now have their say,
Yet somehow I've constructed
A throne for my display.

Reports of grand design,
Say I've made a mess,
But in this maze of marvels,
My clumsy turns impress.

Secrets in the Spaces Between

In the gaps of thought so wild,
Lies a treasure trove undrawn,
With winks from goofy moments,
Awkward truths now dawn.

I trip over my own wisdom,
Like shoes on the wrong track,
Yet laughter fills the silence,
As I try to find my knack.

Hidden jesters in the air,
Whispers laugh and prance,
For when I seek perfection,
They lead me in a dance.

So here's a toast to foolishness,
In every bumbling scene,
Because the best of life's secrets,
Are found in spaces unseen.

Fragments of a Forgotten Thesis

Once I had a grand idea,
Piled high upon my desk,
But pages turned to paper airplanes,
Lost amidst the jest.

The notes are all a jumble,
The genius turned to goo,
Yet every scribble laughs aloud,
At plans I thought I knew.

With coffee stains like constellations,
And snacks amidst the prose,
I scribbled down a symphony,
Of chaos that just grows.

So here I sit in wonder,
Crafting gold from pure dismay,
For in these funny fragments,
Are fragments of my play.

Lost and Found in the Mundane

I made a sandwich, what a delight,
But I forgot the bread, what a sight!
I searched my pockets, two socks and a key,
But no sign of crust, oh dear, woe is me!

My coffee's gone cold, I meant to sip,
Instead, I just stared, lost in thoughts that skip.
The TV's on mute, yet it clearly mocks,
As I fumble with puzzles and unmatching socks.

The cat's in my lap, giving me sass,
I lost all my plans, like a pass in class.
In the chaos of life, I joke and I grin,
Perhaps my manual's lost in the din.

Oh, how I tumble through daily routines,
Like a jester in life, with chortles and scenes.
If laughter's the key, then I'll find my way,
In this loony circus of mundane ballet.

Navigating Life's Ambiguities

I opened a jar, what chaos ensued,
Spices exploded, oh, how they stewed!
The recipe's vague, like a riddle or game,
Why is my dinner now poking in shame?

My GPS failed, it led me astray,
I took the wrong turn, then I lost the day.
Left at the apple, or was it a tree?
I should've just asked, maybe it's just me.

In the land of the puzzled, I grin and I sigh,
An umbrella for sun? Well, why not, oh my!
With mismatched instructions tucked deep in my brain,
I dance with confusion, don't mind the terrain.

Yet here I stand, just a jester at heart,
Chasing my whims, oh, where do I start?
In the trials of life, there's a chuckle to find,
For each little hiccup, a grin interlined.

A Compass for the Unprepared

Maps are confusing, they twist and they sway,
   I navigate life like a boat gone astray.
  A signpost to nowhere, pure chaos ahead,
Who put these two roads in my book of dread?

With a hat on my head that's way too offbeat,
I wander the sidewalks with shoes on my feet.
A guidebook with riddles, and none with solutions,
  How did I sign up for these wild substitutions?

The washing machine sings an off-key refrain,
  As I tumble through cycles, it drives me insane!
I find socks that match, and then lose them again,
  Is this life's grand joke, or just missing a pen?

  At the end of my quest, I chuckle a bit,
With a compass that points to a fun little skit.
  In this circus of life, I may spin and twirl,
With laughter as my guide, let confusion unfurl.

When Logic Loses Its Way

I set out to clean, but the couch called my name,
With a snack in my hand, it's a frivolous game.
The dust bunnies laughed, they just wouldn't flee,
As I danced with distractions so blissfully free.

I tried to be serious, put on my best face,
But a cat in a box just brightens the place.
Phone in one hand, and my coffee in two,
What was I doing? Oh right, I had to brew!

Logic went missing, quite lost on the trail,
Like a ship made of jelly, that's bound to derail.
In the mess of the day, I find laughter the key,
When logic's a joke, life's a grand comedy.

So here's to the chaos, the laughs we will share,
When plans go awry, and we simply don't care.
With joy in the journey, let's lead the parade,
In this world of confusion, let chuckles cascade.

Silence of the Unwritten

In the chaos of the day, we hide,
Dancing to a script that's been denied.
No instructions in sight, just a grin,
Oh, the fun of guessing what's next to begin.

Lost in laughter, we take the leap,
With every misstep, a promise to keep.
Who needs a guide when we trip and fall?
We write our own rules, as we bumble through it all.

Each bump is a chapter, a tale of delight,
We sip our confusion, it tastes just right.
With playful hearts, we tumble and roll,
In a world with no manual, we revel in the soul.

So toast to the errors, the goof and the gaffe,
For it's in our blunders we create the best laugh.
A life without rules may seem rather grim,
But with laughter as compass, we'll never grow dim.

The Weft of Chance and Choice

A map unfolds, but it's all a joke,
Paths wander wildly, and that's how we poke.
With choices to make and whims to embrace,
We bounce off the walls, a silly rat race.

Taking the left when the right seems so bright,
Every detour, a twist, keeps the vibe light.
Who knew the path would lead to that cake?
In the world of mishaps, new memories we make.

The compass spins wildly, what's north, what's south?
We follow our noses, then life gives a shout.
A fork in the road, a snack in between,
Each step is a laugh, our journey's unseen.

So let's raise a glass to the fences we break,
In a dance of chance, our hearts always awake.
For when it's all random, we laugh through the noise,
In the web of the unseen, we find our true joys.

Haphazard Wisdom

They say that life should come with some rules,
But we're just a bunch of giggling fools.
With wisdom uncharted, we flow like a breeze,
The secrets we find are a jumbled tease.

Stumbling on gems hidden deep in the dirt,
In the mess of our lives, we might get a spurt.
The lessons we learn from accidental falls,
We chuckle together, our laughter enthralls.

For what's an adventure without some wild turns?
With each misplaced step, a new lesson learns.
No guides are required in this circus of fate,
We juggle our missteps, never feeling late.

Let's toast to confusion, the quirks of the soul,
In the land of the lost, we still remain whole.
In this muddled parade, we giggle and roam,
With haphazard wisdom, we've crafted our home.

The Carefree Traveler's Log

Packed up my bags with a dash of flair,
No itinerary planned, just fresh mountain air.
With snacks in the trunk and a map upside down,
Off I go joyful, with no hint of a frown.

Each stop is a story, a laugh, or a spill,
Got lost in a field, but it's part of the thrill.
My GPS whispers, but it won't keep me straight,
For wandering aimlessly is just too great.

From coffee shop chats to the lost and found place,
I've made a few friends—each with a unique face.
We share silly tales over pancakes and tea,
Every misfortune turns to pure jubilee.

So here's to the road, unpaved and unclear,
With each twist and turn, I hold laughter near.
For in the travel of life's uncharted log,
I'll scribble my joy, dancing through every fog.

The Anatomy of Uncertainty

In a world of twists and quirks,
Who knew life would be so berserk?
With a phone in hand, I still feel lost,
Mapping out paths comes at a cost.

Instructions scribbled on napkin paper,
Should I follow or risk a caper?
The GPS fails, it gives a sigh,
Guess I'll improvise and just try!

A recipe scribbled, half-formed thoughts,
Mixing life like I mix my pots.
A pinch of courage, a dash of dread,
Hope someone checks on me instead!

Each step I take, a dance on toes,
Who left the breadcrumbs? No one knows!
Yet laughter rings amidst the strife,
Unwritten rules make up this life.

Dilemmas Without Directions

In the kitchen, a pot starts to boil,
I wonder, is this how chefs toil?
With no recipe for soup or stew,
I guess I'll add whatever's in view!

The map says straight, but I took a turn,
Lost in thought, oh, how I yearn.
Each detour leads to new surprise,
Like finding tacos in a pie!

The clock ticks loud—what time is it, friend?
I'll consult my watch; oh wait, it's on trend!
So here I stand, no clear way,
Just wandering like a lost bouquet.

It's part of the fun, or so they say,
When every choice feels like a play.
Life's a party, no need for plans,
Just grab a drink and make some fans!

Handwritten Notes from Tomorrow

Yesterday's scribbles, a jumbled mess,
Tomorrow's chaos I clearly guess.
Notes from a future I barely see,
Adventures waiting, just for me!

Who wrote this stuff? Was it a prank?
A picture of me, and a turtle's tank?
I must be wild or perhaps just bold,
To chase after stories that need to be told.

Spilled coffee marks and random doodles,
Circling words like unruly poodles.
Each line a puzzle that makes me grin,
A treasure map to where I begin!

In this mess, there's beauty too,
A mix of laughter, a sprinkle of blue.
Each note a chuckle, a chance to play,
In the circus of life, let's play all day!

Searching for the Blueprint of Being

I thought I'd find a chart or guide,
But life keeps secrets—there's no pride.
With laughter close, I tread the line,
Following whims; they're often divine!

Lost my way on the path of fate,
Is that a detour, or just a wait?
Plans are fickle, might bend and sway,
Just like my hair on a messy day!

The rhythm of nonsense plays in my head,
A jiggle of joy, can't be misled.
Let's dance on the edge of the unknown,
With each silly step, we're never alone.

So here we are, in this grand charade,
With laughter and quirks, we're perfectly made.
No blueprint required; just follow the fun,
In the chaos of life, we've already won!

Life Between the Lines

I woke up today, hair like a bird,
Looked in the mirror, thought, that's absurd.
Coffee spills, the toast takes a dive,
Do I need a manual to survive?

At work, the printer starts to jam,
My boss walks in, and I go 'Oh, damn!'
Emails pinging, phone calls galore,
If only instructions came with this chore.

Out on the street, someone trips over air,
I can't help but laugh, it's just not fair.
Life's a circus, with a clown as a guide,
If laughter's the answer, let's enjoy the ride!

So here's to the chaos, the messes we make,
With each goofy moment, we learn and awake.
We squint at the map, but it leads us to fun,
Turns out it's the journey, not just the run.

Dance of the Uncertainty

Two left feet in a waltzing spree,
I'm stepping on toes, oh mercy me!
The music's an odd mix, a strange little tune,
I dance like a duck, under a bright moon.

The clock's ticking fast, I'm late for the show,
But I trip on a banana, and go with the flow.
Instructions elusive, like clouds in the sky,
Just wing it, they say, and I'll tell you why.

With each little wobble, I'm finding my beat,
Life's more of a jig than a shuffle retreat.
Embrace the missteps, let your heart lead the way,
Who needs a manual when you've got a sway?

So let's spin around, get tangled in fun,
This dance of the unsure is never quite done.
In the whirlwind of laughter, we joyfully sway,
For it's laughter and love that will guide our display.

Embracing the Unfathomable

Out in the world where logic takes leave,
I'm trying to tackle whatever I believe.
Today it's a puzzle, tomorrow a game,
Why's there no handbook for this silly fame?

My cat's got a plan, she's plotting her heist,
While I'm left wondering, how to be nice.
A sneeze, then a laugh, an unexpected spree,
It's chaotic delight, I can already see!

Traffic lights blink like they're lost in a trance,
Is this a commute or a surreal dance?
With every red signal, I rethink my role,
Perhaps life's just an improv, with a pinch of soul.

So here we are, in this curious mess,
No rulebook in hand, just a moment to guess.
Let's toast to the weird, the wild, and the free,
For embracing the unknown is just how it should be.

Lessons on the Fickle Breeze

A breeze rolls in, with secrets to share,
It whispers and giggles, a wild little dare.
Today's weather is sunny, but who made that guess?
I'm caught in flip-flops, life's little dress.

Oh winds of confusion, you play tag with my hat,
I chase it through puddles, make quite a splat.
Do the clouds hold the answers, or just more surprise?
Umbrellas are fickle, with sarcastic ties.

The trees start to sway, like they're in on the joke,
Each rustle a riddle, each branch a spoke.
I laugh at the chaos, it's way more my style,
Forget the instructions, let's roam free for a while!

Each gust brings a lesson that can't be confined,
In the dance of the breeze, a truth you will find.
To live without manuals, with hearts open wide,
Is the greatest adventure, let's take it in stride.

The Rulebook in My Mind

In the attic of thoughts, a book's gone awry,
Pages are missing, oh me, oh my!
Rules scribbled in crayon, they're quite hard to see,
I stumble and bumble, no clue where to be.

Each chapter's a riddle, a puzzle, a test,
I laugh at the chaos, I must confess.
Instructions unclear, but I'm having some fun,
Life's like a game, but the rules are all gone.

My tea is in two cups, my socks mismatched,
I once had a plan, then it got detached.
A foot in the fridge, my head in the clouds,
This manual's missing; I can't hear the crowds.

So I dance through the mess, with joy and a grin,
Taking every curveball like a wild violin.
In the book that I lack, it seems I'm the star,
In a comedy show, with a laugh that's bizarre.

Undefined Paths of Existence

Bumbling through life like a blindfolded mime,
Each step is a riddle, a rhythm, a rhyme.
With no GPS and no clue to my quest,
I'm tumbling through nothing; oh, isn't this jest!

I tripped on a thought, fell into surprise,
My hat's now a fishbowl; is that wise?
Paths twist and turn, like noodles in soup,
With laughter as my guide, I'll just join the troop.

A detour to bliss, I get lost in the fun,
Each misstep a lesson, a joke just begun.
No map in my pocket, but I'll surely explore,
The wacky absurd, who could ask for more?

With giggles as compass, I wander and roam,
In this land of folly, I've crafted a home.
Undefined, yet alive, in laughter I thrive,
In the chaos of living, I feel so alive!

A Compass Without a Needle

A compass in hand, but the needle is gone,
It spins in a circle, sings a silly song.
To the north or the south, who can really tell?
I'm lost in the giggles, oh isn't it swell?

The sun is my helper, or so I assume,
It's shining its light, but it's stuck in my room.
With every wrong turn, I'm still full of cheer,
The journey is wild, and I'm far from austere.

This map's just a doodle, all squiggly lines,
My directions are jumbled like mismatched designs.
Yet here I am laughing, with joy in my chest,
For traveling's fun when you're guessing the rest.

I'll waltz with the breeze, let the whimsy decide,
In this quest for the unknown, I've nothing to hide.
Call me a dreamer, a fool on the roam,
But a heart full of laughter is the best kind of home!

Navigating Chaos: A Guide

To navigate life is a dance full of bends,
With chaos as partner, we twist with no ends.
The steps are all jumbled, the rhythm awry,
But what's life without giggles? Oh, wouldn't we cry!

I throw out the rulebook, it's gathering dust,
In this adventure, it's laughter I trust.
With marshmallows as maps, and confetti as drew,
I'll wade through the whirlwind, with joy as my crew.

Mistakes are just sprinkles on cakes of delight,
I'll juggle my blunders with all of my might.
With each slip and trip, I sprinkle some cheer,
For the madness of life is what keeps it so dear.

So grab your own compass, though needles may stray,
Join me in this circus, we'll find our own way.
Through laughter and chaos, we'll prance and we'll glide,

In this wild, funny journey, come take a wild ride!

Theometer of Unlived Dreams

I set my goals like shooting stars,
But all I get are laughing bars.
With every plan I try to scheme,
It seems to vanish like a dream.

I question fate, it's such a joke,
My life's a riddle, just a hoax.
Like laundry socks that disappear,
I wonder if the end is near.

Each wish I cast, a puff of smoke,
The universe just loves to poke.
I sip my tea and scratch my head,
Where's the guide for dreams unsaid?

I laugh and dance in blissful glee,
No roadmap shows what's meant to be.
In every tumble, twist, and turn,
It's mishaps that I've come to learn.

The Case of the Missing Instructions

I opened boxes filled with glee,
But found each piece a mystery.
The screws are round, the bolts are square,
Instructions vanished in thin air.

I followed steps, or so I thought,
But ended up with something odd.
A chair that wobbles, a table bright,
It's a circus act, what a sight!

With crayons marking every page,
I've turned my life into a stage.
No clues to clear this messy plot,
Just laughter at the things I've bought.

Yet through the chaos, I must confess,
My heart finds joy in this great mess.
Each failed attempt is one more laugh,
In this quirky, winding path.

Unfurling the Uncharted

A map was drawn with colors bright,
But all it leads to sheer delight.
With every twist, a brand new chance,
Life's clumsy turn becomes a dance.

I wander off the beaten track,
Embrace the goofiness I lack.
A compass spinning, what a sight,
I'm stumbling into pure delight.

Each page I turn is blank and bold,
With tales of mishaps yet untold.
I'll write my rules, no need for guides,
In this wild ride, my spirit glides.

So here's to all the fun we seek,
With every twist, the joy's unique.
In laughter's grip, we dance anew,
No map required for this review.

Tumultuous Pages of Life

The book of life is filled with quirks,
With chapters where each chaos lurks.
I flip through pages, more than a few,
Wondering where the plotline flew.

Comedies and dramas intertwine,
Mistakes that sparkle, oh so divine.
I stumble through this written prose,
Amidst the giggles, I strike a pose.

The ending's fuzzy, plots collide,
With every twist, I take in stride.
In every trial, a punch line found,
In turbulent waves, I'm blissfully drowned.

So let's misread with giddy zest,
Embrace the mess—it's for the best.
In joyful paces, let time unravel,
For life's the best one-act travel.

The Missing User's Guide

I opened the box, what's all this stuff?
Instructions vague, is that a snuff?
Two parts here, one part there,
Building this thing? I'm in despair.

Wires everywhere, it's like a nest,
What's the black cord? What's the best?
Do I twist it? Do I tape?
I might just need a whole new shape!

It beeps and whirs, gives a little sputter,
Caught in a mess, this is what's the matter.
It pours itself tea, then starts to sing,
My toaster's gone mad, what's next? A fling?

Maybe it's time for a good retreat,
Researching manuals, I admit defeat.
To the internet I flee in fright,
Lost in translation; someone, hold me tight!

Echoes of Uncharted Territories

Set forth on a quest, what's the ultimate goal?
With a guide in my hand, but it's made of coal.
Maps fold up like they're from a horror tale,
Every turn I take seems to end in hail.

I ask for directions, get glances and stares,
The locals just chuckle, but nobody cares.
"Go left at the llama, then right by the fog,"
I scribble in notes, this feels like a slog.

I've lost my sense, my very own way,
Navigating life is like solo ballet.
Too many spins, get tangled up tight,
The dance card is full, it's a comical sight.

Yet still I march on, we'll conquer this land,
A treasure awaits, it's just unplanned.
With laughter and giggles, I'll make it through,
Adventure's a riot, who needs a clue?

The Puzzle Without a Picture

A jigsaw of life with no edges in sight,
Pieces that clash, yet they feel just right.
Searching for corners, not quite in the frame,
Why do they fit? It seems oh so lame.

Colors don't match, and they curve in strange ways,
My brain starts to smoke in this puzzle maze.
Frustration's a friend, a quirky delight,
It's like deciphering a dog's bark at night.

Up is down, and left gets confused,
Solving this riddle is nothing but bruised.
But here comes the laughter, it lightens the weight,
It's joy in the chaos, let's celebrate fate!

So I scramble and hop, with gusto I play,
In a world of mismatches, I'll find my way.
For in every odd piece, a story unfolds,
What fun it is to create without molds!

Clueless Journeys

Packed up my car with a full tank of hope,
What's this route? They didn't give me scope.
Siri's in stitches; she starts to mislead,
"You've got twenty miles!" I scream in plead.

A road sign's mangling, it points everywhere,
Like a game of charades, it's filled with flair.
Left or right? Who can really tell?
I end up in places where lost folks dwell.

The coffee shop there says "You're far from home,"
Tears mingled with laughter, guess I can roam.
So, roll down the window, let the fresh air in,
This clueless journey is where I begin.

With every wrong turn, a lesson bestowed,
In this wacky trip, the laughter has flowed.
So here's to detours and plans all awry,
Life's better uncharted; here's to the why!

www.ingramcontent.com/pod-product-compliance
Lightning Source LLC
Chambersburg PA
CBHW051654160426
43209CB00004B/890